The
Outer Banks

THE
OUTER BANKS

BILL YENNE

The
Globe
Pequot
Press

Produced by American Graphic Systems, Inc.

Text © 1998 Bill Yenne. Design ©1998 American Graphic Systems, Inc.

Designed and captioned by Bill Yenne, with design assistance by Azia Yenne.
Proofreading by Joan B. Hayes.

All photographs are by Bruce Roberts, with the following exceptions:
AGS Archives: 6, 12
Carolinas Golf Group, LLC: 16
Carteret County Tourism Development Bureau: 2, 43, 44, 45, 46, 47
Dare County Tourism Bureau, Mike Booher: 5, 7, 10, 22, 27
Elizabethan Gardens: 28, 29

Cover photograph: Currituck Beach Lighthouse.
Page one photograph: Delicate shells on the beach at Cape Hatteras.
Page two photograph: A young snorkler at Cape Lookout.

Library of Congress Cataloging -in- Publication Data is available.
ISBN 0-7627-0384-9
Manufactured in Canada
First Edition / First Printing

Welcome to the Outer Banks

The Outer Banks of North Carolina are a magical place of sand and sun where a southeast breeze blows gently and an occasional northeast storm blows in to refresh and clear the air. The Outer Banks are a recreational wonderland, attracting numerous visitors every year who come to enjoy the surfing, windsurfing, fishing and hang gliding. Others come simply to stroll the many miles of unspoiled beaches collecting seashells and exploring five centuries of shipwrecks. A birdwatcher's paradise, the Outer Banks provide a variety of habitats and are a valuable wintering area for migrating waterfowl.

Two national seashores, Cape Hatteras and Cape Lookout, offer a wide variety of activities, from birding to boating and from fishing to folklore, as well as an opportunity to see and to explore several of the largest and most important lighthouses in the United States.

In The Early Days

It was on the Outer Banks in 1497 that Amerigo Vespucci first set foot on the continent which bears his name. French and Spanish sailors followed in those footsteps, but no one came to stay until 1584, when Queen Elizabeth I of England (*above*) issued a charter to Sir Walter Raleigh to establish a colony here. After several preliminary explorations, a settlement was established on Roanoke Island in 1587 by a small group of hearty souls, including the artist John White. It was the first English-speaking colony in the New World.

As provisions began to run short, White sailed for England on a resupply mission. When he was finally able to return to the Outer Banks in 1590, he discovered that the Roanoke Colony and its small population had disappeared with no trace but the strange word "Croatoan" carved on a tree. The mystery has never been solved, even to this day.

The Lost Colony

When it opened at Roanoke Island's Waterside Theater on the evening of July 4, 1937, Paul Green's outdoor drama *The Lost Colony* was scheduled to run for just one season. No one could have predicted that it would continue to be staged for sell-out crowds every summer since, entertaining over three million theater-goers, and earning Green a Pulitzer Prize.

The Lost Colony weaves the tale of the trials and tribulations of Sir Walter Raleigh's ill-fated Roanoke Colony, its people and their relations with the Native Americans who had lived on the Outer Banks and the surrounding area for centuries before John White and his colonists built their first cabins in these beautiful lands.

Green conceived the drama as a 350th anniversary tribute to the birth of John White's granddaughter, Virginia Dare, who was the first English child born in the New World.

The Graveyard of the Atlantic

The ancient oak skeletons that can be seen in the shifting sand of the Outer Banks are a silent reminder of days gone by, of hidden dangers and the reason why the coast of North Carolina is known as "the Graveyard of the Atlantic." It is off the Banks that the cold waters of the Labrador Current meet the warm Gulf Stream, creating dangerous currents.

Over 600 ships have been wrecked here since the sixteenth century, including the famous ironclad warship *Monitor*, which was lost in a storm in 1862. During both world wars, German submarines also lurked in the waters off the Outer Banks — known then as "Torpedo Junction" — and their prey added to the total.

Several of the lost vessels still remain as an intriguing part of the landscape for beachcombers on the Outer Banks, while others offshore are popular with divers.

Currituck Beach Lighthouse

Located in a wooded area near the small town of Corolla, the 158-foot Currituck Beach Lighthouse is the northernmost of the famous Outer Banks lighthouses. With its light visible for 20 miles, it was constructed in 1875 to illuminate the dark midpoint between the lighthouses located 40 miles north at Cape Henry, Virginia and 40 miles south at Bodie Island.

Each of the other lighthouses on the Outer Banks had been painted in a particular pattern to allow them to act as a navigation aid in daylight, but the Currituck Beach Lighthouse was left in its natural red brick color, and this became its unique point of recognition.

No longer essential to navigators, the Currituck Lighthouse is open to the public seasonally. Visitors can climb the interior steel staircase and view the entrance area where the lightkeepers once stockpiled whale oil to light the lamps.

Amid the Drifting Dunes

The dunes running north and south of Currituck Lighthouse and the small town of Corolla offer a wonderful world of solitude and an opportunity to be close to nature. With the Atlantic Ocean no more than a mile to the east, and Currituck Sound a similar distance to the west, one has the feeling of being cut off from the cares and hassles of the everyday world. This area was not connected to electricity lines until the 1950s, and the bridge that connects the Outer Banks to the mainland was not built until 1958. Currituck Outer Banks was not connected to line-distributed electricity until the 1950s. Today, the road stops at Corolla, but before 1984 there wasn't even a road *to* Corolla.

The 1,800-acre Currituck National Wildlife Refuge, located a few miles from the Currituck Lighthouse, is home to endangered plants, wild boar and Corolla's famous wild horses.

Sunset on the Shore at Duck

It is hard to imagine a more tranquil place to enjoy a summer sunset. South of Corolla, at one of the narrowest points on the Outer Banks is the town of Duck, whose many comfortable vacation homes are popular with people who come to the area to relax with the sand, the sea and the sunsets.

The town takes its name from the waterfowl who pass this way, and which were once an important part of the livelihood for folks hereabouts. Farm produce and wild fowl were once shipped by schooner up the inland waterway to Norfolk and then transshipped to New York, Washington, Boston and Philadelphia. A half century ago, the shallow draft steamer *Comet* ran past Duck from Popular Branch on the mainland, to Aydlett, Knotts Island and north to Virginia as far as Norfolk. On return trips it brought the goods that would stock the shelves of Outer Banks general stores.

The Winds of Kitty Hawk

On December 17, 1903, history was made at a place called Kill Devil Hills near the Outer Banks town of Kitty Hawk. At 10:35 that morning, Orville Wright lay down prone across the bottom wing of a two-winged contraption that he built with his brother, Wilbur, and grasped the controls.

With a small engine sputtering noisily, he coaxed the machine into the air. History's first powered flight of a heavier-than-air machine carrying a person lasted 12 seconds, with Orville covering 120 feet. By the end of the day, each of the brothers had made two successful flights, with Wilbur covering 852 feet in his last turn at the controls. Because of the strong, steady winds on the Banks, the Wrights had been testing gliders here each autumn for three years.

Today, the huge granite Wright Brothers Memorial Pylon (*opposite*) commemorates the events that took place here.

Golf at Nag's Head

To the south of Kitty Hawk is the community of Nag's Head and the par 71 Nag's Head Golf Links, a true Scottish links-style course, which opened in 1988.

Today, the town of Kitty Hawk, which served as the base for Wilbur and Orville Wright during their legendary experiments with gliders and powered aircraft in 1900-1903 is today a popular destination for tourists and vacationers.

The name is derived from the Native American word "Chickahauk," which translates as "the goose-hunting area," and whose pronunciation probably sounded like "Kitty Hawk" to the early English settlers. Although the Wright brothers' first flight took place four miles away, at Kill Devil Hills, Kitty Hawk is associated with the great event, because the telegraph message announcing it was transmitted from Kitty Hawk and carried the town's dateline.

Nag's Head

Nameplates from ships lost off the Outer Banks bear testimony to the nautical history of Nag's Head. As the story goes, the town was named by English sailors after a high point on the Scilly Islands, which was the last sight of their homeland that they saw as they set sail for America.

Legend also tells that the pirate Blackbeard, who occasionally landed near here during the eighteenth century, was outdone in piracy by the folks of Nag's Head, who tied lanterns to their horses at night, and walked them up and down the shore to fool ships into thinking the horses were other ships off shore. As the real ships changed course and ran aground, their spilled cargo became easy pickings. By the 1830s, Nag's Head became the resort area that it has remained. Today, comfortable accommodations and seasonal rentals greet visitors who come for the beaches, fishing, golfing and cool Atlantic breezes.

Jockey's Ridge State Park

The Wright brothers did not come to the Outer Banks from Dayton, Ohio by accident, and they didn't come for the fishing. They carefully scrutinized US Weather Bureau data for the entire country and chose the Outer Banks for the strong, steady breeze that was perfect for testing their gliders.

Though their first powered flight is best remembered, Wilbur and Orville had already made over a thousand glider flights on these dunes. Today, the breezes still blow over what is considered to be one of the best hang-gliding spots anywhere. The 110-foot dunes at Jockey's Ridge State Park, near Nag's Head and Kill Devil Hills, are the largest on the East Coast. Northeast and southwest winds blow the sand back and forth, keeping it from blowing away. The views are breathtaking, as is the hike up the dunes on a hot day. The dunes are a favorite place for kite flying, as well as for hang gliding.

Surf Fishing

The Outer Banks may be the best place on the East Coast of North America for surf fishing. No license or permit is required for saltwater fishing, but freshwater fishing does require a North Carolina fishing license.

A favored surf fishing area is the 70 miles of barrier islands that comprise the Cape Hatteras National Seashore. The "Park" as local people call it, is a fascinating combination of natural and cultural resources, and provides a wide variety of recreational opportunities other than fishing.

Here, the winds can range from gentle southwest breezes to strong northeast storm winds. The summer days are usually warm and humid, and are often punctuated by fast-moving, severe thunderstorms. Winter temperatures are usually cool, although the wind can get quite cold, and spring and fall days can vary a great deal between these two extremes.

Alone with the Surf and a Fishing Rod

Surf fishing on the Outer Banks includes the Atlantic Ocean, of course, and the sounds as well. Located to the west of the Banks, Pamlico Sound is the largest inland body of water on the East Coast, and one of the richest saltwater fishing grounds anywhere. North of Roanoke Island, Currituck Sound also supports freshwater species such as bass.

In addition to surf fishing, Outer Banks fishermen also avail themselves of the eight public fishing piers on the coast between Kitty Hawk and Cape Hatteras. These include Kitty Hawk Pier, Avalon Fishing Pier, Nag's Head Fishing Pier, Jennette's Fishing Pier, Outer Banks Pier Fishing Center, Hatteras Island Fishing Pier, Avon Fishing Pier and Cape Hatteras Fishing Pier. They say that the best time for pier fishing is in the fall, and most piers are open from April through November. Bait, tackle and ice are generally available near all the piers.

A Good Day's Catch

A fishing trip to the shores of the Outer Banks holds the promise of ocean grey trout (*seen here*), as well as spot, croaker, snapper, bluefish, flounder, channel bass, largemouth bass, cobia, bonito, sea mullet, spot bluefish, tuna and amberjack, as well as red and black drum.

Beginning in March and continuing through the summer, bass, flounder, sea mullet, spot, bluefish, trout and croaker are a typical catch from both pier and surf fishing, while inshore on Pamlico Sound and Currituck Sound, flounder are plentiful and speckled trout can be caught around structures and in the adjacent marshes.

Flounder can be caught oceanside or soundside, and cobia are good spring catches in the sounds. In April, people start to fish for largemouth bass in the Currituck Sound. During the summer, Spanish mackerel can also be fished from shore.

The Home of World Record Fishing

The Atlantic waters off the Outer Banks offer great fishing from boat or shore. Outer Banks fishermen hold the all-tackle record for blue marlin, with a 1,142-pounder that was caught in 1974. Meanwhile, a Banker earned a world record in 1972 with a 31 pound, 12 ounce bluefish.

Ocean fishing off the Banks changes with the season. In the early spring, offshore ocean fishing is particularly good for sheepshead, tarpon and yellowfin tuna and flounder. As the ocean water gets warmer in the late spring and early summer, the cobia move out into the Atlantic from Pamlico Sound.

The best blue marlin fishing is in June, and by August, the pompano, bigeye tuna and wahoo move toward the Outer Banks. In the fall, bluefish over 15 pounds are common, often running with bluefin tuna. If you go out by boat, king mackerel are often the reward for a great offshore adventure.

The Incredible Blue Crab

Named for the color of their hind legs, blue crabs are one of the quintessential delicacies of the Outer Banks. A crab feast on a long, leisurely afternoon or evening is a favorite pastime for visitors and "Bankers" alike.

The upper surface of the crab shell is bluish to dark green to brownish-green in color. The fingers of the claws of males are blue, tipped with red; the female claws are red with darker red tips. The lower body surfaces are creamy-white or white. Blue crabs are found in abundance in Chesapeake Bay and along the Atlantic and Gulf coasts. People catch the crabs using dip nets or open traps. The latter is a weighted trap that lies flat with bait on the floor of the trap. When crabs go to the bait, lines are drawn, the sides go up and the trap is pulled with the crabs enclosed. Baited traps favored by commercial fishermen are also used by recreational crabbers.

Heading Out for Crab

A day of crabbing on Albemarle Sound begins early with a boat trip to what are hoped to be good crabbing grounds. When the crabber reaches the right spot, the crab traps are thrown into the water, each one attached to a buoy marked to distinguish it from those of other crabbers.

The commercial crabbers use baited traps, many of which are now made with plastic-coated, galvanized wire for longer life. These traps have funnel-shaped "doors," through which the crabs crawl to get to the bait. When the crab is inside, it cannot readily escape. The crabber will pull the traps at regular intervals and remove the crabs through a hinged door. If crabbing is good at a particular location, the trap will be rebaited and returned to the water. Commercial crabbers also use trot lines, stout lines with pieces of bait which are laid on the bottom and also marked with buoys. The line is pulled into the boat with the crabs.

From Sound to Table

Many of the crabs caught commercially during a cool, misty morning on one of the sounds will be on the menu at one of the many Outer Banks seafood restaurants by lunchtime. A traditional way to eat crab is for a group of people to gather around a large table covered with brown paper with a large bucket of freshly cooked crab in the middle.

Although the early English settlers — and the Native Americans before them — fished these waters, commercial fishing such as we know it today, probably dates to the 1880s. Zeke Daniels, a local postmaster and fisherman, is credited with starting the first commercial fishing operation on Roanoke Island in a town he named Wanchese after one of the two Native Americans whom Sir Walter Raleigh took to England in 1594. The town of Manteo was already named for the second of the two men, so it was an obvious choice.

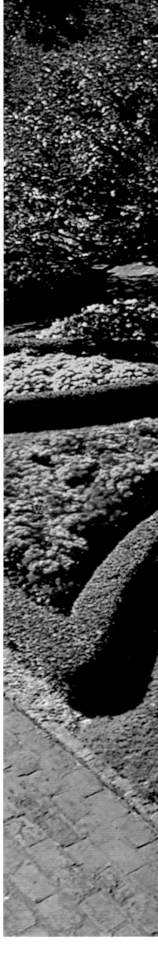

Elizabethan Gardens

Located in the town of Manteo, in a tranquil setting on the shores of Roanoke Sound, the Elizabethan Gardens were designed by the great landscape architects Umberto Innocenti and Richard Webel to commemorate Sir Walter Raleigh's efforts to colonize the New World during the reign of Queen Elizabeth I. These lovely English-style gardens are a year-round mecca for horticulturists and all visitors who enjoy beautiful flowers.

Masses of blooming azaleas, dogwoods, rhododendrons, vines, herbs, bulbs and spring annuals peak around the middle of April. Sweet-scented gardenias, roses, magnolias, myrtle, lilies, hydrangeas and summer annuals reach their height of bloom in July (*above*). Riotous summer bedding plants, hibiscus, chrysanthemums (*right*) and impatiens are featured in the autumn months, while camellias are in bloom from late fall through the winter, until March.

The Elizabeth II

On the Outer Banks, one is never far from a reminder of the area's rich history. The arrival of the first English settlers is brought to life dramatically by the *Elizabeth II*, a reproduction of a sixteenth century square-rigged sailing vessel such as Sir Walter Raleigh used to sail to America in 1585.

Berthed at the Elizabeth II State Historic Park on Manteo's picturesque waterfront, the vessel was built to commemorate the New World's Quadricentennial, and was given to the state of North Carolina in 1984. The *Elizabeth II*, which is considered to be an accurate reproduction in every possible detail, is open for guided tours.

Once aboard the *Elizabeth II*, visitors may view a video program describing life aboard a sixteenth century ship, and in the summer season, living history interpreters portray mariners and colonists from Raleigh's voyages.

Taking The Ferry

Just as with the English pioneers four centuries ago, a great deal of travel to and from the Outer Banks today is on the water. In fact, until the bridges were built, the only way to get to the Banks was by boat, usually by private boat.

Ocracoke Island is still isolated from the mainland and served only by boat. Entrepreneurs began offering ferry service across the Oregon Inlet between Hatteras Island and Bodie Island in the 1920s, and in 1947, the North Carolina Department of Transportation Ferry Service began offering a regularly-scheduled vehicle and passenger ferry system throughout the Outer Banks.

Today, this year-round service serves 14 points throughout the region, with trips that range from 20 minutes between Hatteras Island and Ocracoke Island to 150 minutes between Ocracoke and Swan Quarter.

Bodie Island Lighthouse

A few miles south of the entrance to the Cape Hatteras National Seashore, the Bodie Island Lighthouse fills the 80-mile gap between the Currituck Beach Lighthouse and Cape Hatteras Lighthouse.

With its distinctive, bold stripe pattern, the 156-foot Bodie (pronounced "Boddie") Island Lighthouse was constructed in 1872. While the lighthouse tower itself is not now open to visitors, an exhibit about lighthouse families is presented by the National Park Service in the adjacent visitor's center at the restored lightkeeper's house.

Though it is no longer used for navigation, Bodie's powerful light, with its magnificent Fresnel Lens, still flashes its familiar signal: On for two and one half seconds, off for the same interval, on again for the same and then off for 22.5 seconds before beginning the pattern again.

From Rodanthe to Salvo

T he area around the north end of Hatteras Island was once known as Chicamacomico, but in 1874 the US Post Office changed the name to Rodanthe. During the twentieth century, the Rodanthe community evolved as the three towns of Rodanthe proper, Waves and Salvo. These towns survived as tiny pockets of private land in the unspoiled coastline of the Cape Hatteras National Seashore, which was authorized in 1937 and formally established in 1953.

In 1918, history was made here when the lifeboat crews at the Chicamacomico Lifesaving Station made a daring rescue of 42 crewmen from the British tanker *Mirlo*, which had been torpedoed by a German U-Boat offshore. The Chicamacomico Lifesaving Station was one of seven that once existed on the Outer Banks. Today, the lifesaving task is handled by US Coast Guard helicopters rather than hearty volunteers with wooden boats.

Cape Hatteras Lighthouse

The most widely-recognized symbol of the Outer Banks, Cape Hatteras Lighthouse is the tallest in the United States, rising 208 feet from the sandy cape. The familiar "barber pole" striping was actually a mistake. Because the lighthouse presides over the treacherous Diamond Shoals, it was supposed to be painted in a diamond pattern, but work orders were mixed up and the Cape Lookout Lighthouse got the diamond pattern!

Diamond Shoals are shallow sandbars which extend 14 miles out into the ocean off Cape Hatteras.

The Cape Hatteras Lighthouse was completed in 1870, constructed of 1.25 million bricks baked in kilns on the James River in Virginia, delivered by barge to Cape Creek and hauled by oxcart to the building site. Its walls at the base are 14 feet thick, but narrow to eight feet at the top. The lighthouse is, in turn, topped by its distinctive iron superstructure.

Looking out to Sea

Cape Hatteras Lighthouse, with its original Fresnel lens, was visible 20 miles out to sea. This masterpiece of glass-maker's art has been replaced by modern optics and quartz lighting, but they can extend the beacon's visibility to just 24 miles.

The lighthouse is open to the public from early April until mid-October, and visitors are welcome to climb the 268 steps for a spectacular view of Cape Hatteras. The adjacent lightkeeper's quarters have been restored as a visitors center with displays on the island's maritime history.

The lighthouse was built with no pilings under it, and in recent years the deterioration of the pine foundation has become a serious concern, as the relentless pounding of the Atlantic has become a threat. In the summer of 1996, 300 three-ton sandbags were added around the base of the lighthouse to protect it until a more permanent solution can be found.

Pea Island National Wildlife Refuge

Contained within the Cape Hatteras National Seashore, the Pea Island National Wildlife Refuge was set aside in 1938 to help protect migratory waterfowl. Although the refuge is located in a 12-mile section of Hatteras Island between Oregon Inlet to Rodanthe, its namesake is the wild pea vine which can be seen growing throughout the area.

Within the refuge's 6,000 acres of land and 25,700 acres of boundary water on the Pamlico Sound, more than 265 species of birds make their homes, either permanently or seasonally during migration on the Atlantic Flyway. These include snow geese (*above*), more than 25 species of ducks, tundra swans, herons, egrets, terns and ospreys, as well as laughing gulls, herring gulls and brown pelicans. Observation stations have been constructed, and trails established, so that visitors may watch the birds and wildlife of the area without getting in their way.

Ocracoke Island

Today, 14-mile Ocracoke Island is probably the quietest and most remote corner of the Outer Banks, reachable only by ferry from either the mainland or Hatteras Island. Its history, however, has been lively. Edward Teach, the pirate better known as Blackbeard, had a hideout here, and he was killed in Ocracoke by Lieutenant Robert Maynard in 1718.

Built as a harbor light in 1823, the 75-foot Ocracoke Lighthouse is the second oldest operating American lighthouse. It replaces one built here in 1803 but later destroyed by lightning. The present lens was installed in 1864 to replace the one destroyed in the Civil War.

The small cemetery behind Ocracoke Lighthouse is the final resting place of several seamen who died at sea, including four British sailors killed in 1942 when their ship, the *Bedfordshire*, was hit by a German torpedo.

The Wild Ponies of Ocracoke

Throughout the Outer Banks, one often encounters wild horses. Because the Banks are cut off from the mainland, it is uncertain how they arrived here, but various legends have been circulated. One particularly colorful story about the wild ponies on Ocracoke tells that they are descended from a mating pair of circus horses that survived the sinking of the good ship *Black Squall*, in which all hands and all the other animals died.

Various theories suggest a Spanish origin, given the number of Spanish expeditions that anchored in these waters during the sixteenth century.

The best guess seems to be that the ancestors of today's ponies arrived with Raleigh and the settlers who landed at Roanoke Island and later vanished. The horses on Ocracoke are now within the boundaries of the Cape Hatteras National Seashore, and are protected by the National Park Service.

Cape Lookout

Southof Ocracoke Island is the Cape Lookout National Seashore, a stretch of unspoiled barrier islands which are a wonderland for hikers, beachcombers and fishermen, a place where the mind can wander to embrace local legend.

One of the most intriguing tales that is told around the cape involves a three-masted schooner, *Crissie Wright*. She was coasting north along the North Carolina shore one night in January 1886, when a storm blew in. The captain decided not to try for Diamond Shoals and set sail for Cape Lookout. However, the main mast broke in the wind and the ship was helpless. The waves were too high to launch lifeboats, and the people ashore watching couldn't get their boats through the breakers to help. They watched as the sailors were swept overboard. The following day, the ship's cook was found alive, wrapped in the jib sail. He died a year later, having never fully recovered.

Cape Lookout Lighthouse

Marking the southernmost point of the Outer Banks, Cape Lookout Lighthouse was constructed in 1859 on Core Banks Island. In 1862, during the Civil War, the 156-foot brick tower survived an attempt to blow it up. Its distinctive black diamonds face north and south, while the white ones face east and west. This pattern was actually intended for the Cape Hatteras Light, but were painted here by mistake.

Fully automated since 1950, Cape Lookout was originally built with a Fresnel lamp, but it now features a DCB-24, flashing every 15 seconds to warn of the dreaded Cape Lookout shoals. The beacon is visible for 19 miles.

Maintained jointly by the US Coast Guard and the US National Park Service, Cape Lookout Lighthouse is surrounded by several other structures, including a brick oil house, a coal shed, two cisterns, a summer kitchen and a stable.

A Magical Place

Another perfect day on the Outer Banks comes to a close. The sun sets over Pamlico Sound, gently tinting the clouds over the Atlantic and the sails of a sailing ship offshore. You do a double take. For a moment you are transported in time to the days when Sir Walter Raleigh's settlers arrived.

The Outer Banks are a place that is steeped in history, but they are also a place for the pleasures of today. A morning of beachcombing amid the relics of eighteenth century shipwrecks might be followed by an afternoon of windsurfing. A morning at the Wright Brothers Memorial might be followed by an afternoon of hang gliding over the same dunes where Wilbur and Orville tested their gliders.

Finally, as the sun finally sets and the stars come out, the Cape Hatteras light winks on, casting its reassuring beacon out to sea and down the shore.